PAIN-BEARERS

Compiled by Ann Bird

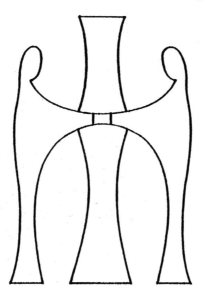

Carry one another's burdens and in this way you will fulfil the law of Christ

Galatians 6:2

The cover photograph was taken on the Mount of Olives. The thorns, thought to be similar to those woven into the crown of thorns placed on Jesus' head, are growing against a high stone wall. Yet just beyond the wall is open countryside and the beautiful Dominus Flevit church built on the spot where Jesus is said to have wept over the city of Jersualem.

(Cover photograph Derek Bird)

PAIN-BEARERS
Compiled by Ann Bird
© Ann Bird 1996

ISBN 1 85852 064 9

CONTENTS

PAIN-BEARERS

'Life-giver, Pain-bearer, Love-maker' – these names for God suggested in Jim Cotter's reflections and prayers, *Healing – More or Less* resonate in the hearts and minds of those who are engaged in the costly ministry of bearing other people's pain day after day. They also speak to those who carry deep pain within themselves and who struggle to survive with courage in the face of what often appears to be a heart-breaking lack of understanding.

This book is intended as an acknowledgement of the emotional pain carers frequently experience as a result of the care they give to others and of the reality of people's individual inner pain. It is also offered as an affirmation that there are positive, resurrection signs to be found in the midst of even the deepest tiredness and despair, and that these serve as a reminder that we are never alone in our bearing of pain. God's healing and transforming love is always present within each apparently unbearable situation. He is, if we allow him so to be, the Life-giver and Love-maker, who, through his nurture and concern, makes our burden of pain bearable.

Clearly we can only look at certain facets of the pain we all have to face and we are not, here, primarily concerned with the physical pain caused by illness which, to a greater or lesser extent, will confront each one of us at some time during our life. The emphasis here is predominantly on the needs of those who are called upon to respond as carers of others. 'Who cares for the carers?' is a question we so often hear. But it is a question to which no easy answers are offered in what follows. Instead this is an attempt to share the experiences and reflections of a few people in differing situations who have found themselves caught up in demanding, caring ministry, who have struggled with the exhaustion of it, who are honest about their own feelings of inadequacy and yet who have insights and encouragement to offer which provide the rest of us with hope.

Ernest Hemingway once wrote that 'we are made strong at the broken places' – the purpose of this book is to help us all towards a greater healing and wholeness, not in *spite* of the pain we bear but *because* of it, not because we can cope in our own strength but because the strength which our Pain-bearing God offers to us is truly made perfect in our weakness.

Ann Bird

BEARING THE WEIGHT OF OTHERS' PAIN IN CIRCUIT MINISTRY

Imagine the scene. 3.55pm on Christmas Eve in a vestry before a Christingle Service which, in a few years, has become a tradition in this particular church. The building is full to overflowing with parents, grandparents and young children and soon they'll all be walking around holding lighted candles! A service of great joy and fun is about to begin and the steward suggests a word of prayer. As she prays the minister's eyes fill with tears and when the steward finishes and looks up she spies the frantic mopping of a wet face.

This was my experience last year and I felt sorry for the steward. She coped remarkably well as I composed myself and explained that things had been getting on top of me. I went into the church and forced myself to lead an excited congregation in Christmas praise. Midnight communion and two services on Christmas Day were easier to cope with and then I could relax and take a few days to think about what had happened in the vestry. Why had I suddenly burst into tears?

In many ways I knew the answer but had not been allowing myself to deal with what was going on.

It really began at the end of my holiday when I was contacted by my colleague to tell me that a young woman in one of my churches had been killed in a road accident. I spoke with the family on the telephone and arranged to see them when I returned. From the moment I got back I was caught up in the grief of the family, the church and the community. The funeral was the day before our twenty-fifth wedding anniversary which was a family celebration.

A few weeks later a friend from another church, who had been at our twenty-fifth 'do', was taken into intensive care. Two weeks later he died.

The telephone rang a week or two later, and the caller was a friend from down the road. Her adopted son had been stabbed to death in a fight. When we first came here he was living with his adoptive parents and his natural sister (a friend of one of my daughters). He came to our Sunday School for a while but eventually left the area when he began to get into trouble with the police and needed special care. He had had an incredibly difficult childhood and in his teenage years went off the rails. He was a nice lad. It was eight weeks before the funeral could proceed, and it eventually took place in mid-December.

Within four weeks of the friend's death in intensive care and during the period of waiting for the young lad's funeral I was notified of another death from the same village as the young woman. Another road accident and a person I had known and spoken to at a recent wedding. His widow and daughters depended heavily on me in the days leading to the funeral which I took in the local Anglican church because our chapel would not accommodate all those expected to attend.

It had been an intense period of pastoral activity overlaying the other work we engage in as superintendent ministers. The events left me emotionally burnt out. I was drained physically, mentally and spiritually.

It was not possible to have an extended rest but I did manage a few days after Christmas and the District retreat in early January. But these were not enough.

The most worrying aspect of how I was now feeling, and something that inevitably got worse, was that I found myself withdrawing from situations of pastoral need. There is a reasonable expectation that I will visit and be involved when needs present themselves. I found that I kept away, almost unconsciously. Even when I recognised what was going on I struggled to respond. All the time you have to deliver the goods on Sundays and at meetings. You somehow keep going, doing what is necessary but without enthusiasm.

Sometimes you are encouraged when people recognise that you have been under a terrific pressure and are concerned for you. Most of the time you feel resentful that people do not seemingly care how you might be feeling. You are fearful too of revealing how you are feeling in case you are labelled a whinger.

In writing this I am not complaining. I accept that my work will involve me in tough times. Yet the expectations of circuits and churches often seem not to recognise just how difficult things can get. If they knew I feel sure that they would want to help relieve the pressures and help you in finding time and space to re-charge your batteries. I had had a sabbatical eighteen months before this series of events took their toll, and I desperately needed another.

By Easter I began to feel a bit better, still knowing that I was working ineffectively, but that I was at least giving the appearance of coping.

In the Easter holidays my father-in-law died suddenly. It was a few weeks after this that I made an appointment to see my GP.

A year on from the first tragedy I am having specific help from the counsellor (free) attached to the surgery. My GP felt that this would help me recognise that I must have rest and refreshment entwined in my working week.

At times I can feel guilty because I know that I have let people down. I do tell people some of what has been happening to me. But mostly they don't want to know that you're not coping. Often they're not coping themselves and you're no use to them if you are having a bad time. Others too, in our congregations are busy, stressed people, in many cases fighting to keep their jobs. And at the bottom line we are ultimately responsible for our own lives and have to accept all that life brings us.

Why have I written this? I'm not really sure. I hope that others in similar circumstances will gain some help from knowing that it is a shared experience. I hope that some will begin to see just how hard ministry is on occasions and that their expectations and demands can be a straw breaking a camel's back.

Anon

> If there is not a place where tears are understood,
> Where can I go to cry?
> If there is not a place where my spirit can take wing,
> Where do I go to fly?
> If there is not a place where my questions can be asked,
> Where do I go to seek?
> If there is not a place where my feelings can be heard
> Where do I go to speak?
> If there is not a place where I can try and learn and grow,
> Where can I just be me?
>
> *Author unknown*

I have to learn and re-learn that I do not have the strength to do all the things I want to do. I am only human and I have very human needs. I need time to myself, I need to pray, to play, to read, to be with friends, to have fun.

If I am always exhausted or working, how can I enter into a healthy, relaxed relationship with people? And if I do not cherish my friendships, how can I expect to keep them? Again and again we religious people forget that we are only human and that we have just the same needs as the people we care for. If we are too proud or stupid or too disorganised to take time out and care for ourselves, who will? And if we fall apart, then who will care for those who depend upon us? Do we not owe it to those we serve to accept our limitations and cherish our minds and bodies so that we will be available to serve them a little longer? I have learned to be very wary of the famous prayer of St Ignatius:

Lord Jesus, teach me to be generous,
To give and not to count the cost,
To fight and not to heed the wounds,
To work and not to seek for rest,
Save in the knowledge that we do your most holy will.

Is it *really* the will of God that we should deny our humanity and work ourselves into the ground? I suspect not. I am not talking about times of disaster or emergency - then surely we are all called to push ourselves to the limits of endurance. No - I am talking of routine, day-to-day caring for the sick, the disabled or otherwise disadvantaged. If we are to be engaged in this work for a substantial number of years then we must take time out, each day, each week and each year. We must take days off and holidays like the rest of men and women because, however dedicated, we remain just that: ordinary men and women.

I say this with some passion because there is a tendency for those on the outside to think that people in the caring professions are somehow different, more dedicated and without ordinary human needs.

Sheila Cassidy

Following the tragic death of a friend of mine, I needed to talk to someone about it. I discovered once again how compelling our need to talk about such things and not just painful events but happy ones as well. It just bursts inside and can't be contained in the narrow, deep solitude of our being.

I looked for someone who had known my friend well, or even a little, to tell them the terrible news; but, in reality, I was just looking for someone with whom to share the pain. This is our profound need - to call out to another and share the burden. Shared suffering always brings a little relief. Again I told myself: Help others to talk. Listen to them quietly, don't worry about saying the right things or saying anything at all. Just be welcoming; people need your support in carrying their pain.

Michel Quoist

'Do not go gentle into that good night.' So wrote Dylan Thomas, the Welsh poet. 'Rage,' he said, 'rage against the dying of the light.' The trouble is that we live in an age in which people have increasingly justified going quite gently and quite passively into more than the good night of death. We have gone a long way in rationalising our way out of ever having to face and work through pain, anxiety or even an occasional sleepless night. Better by far to take the appropriate pill that puts pain and bad moods behind us, the prescription that lets us lie down in limbo for a while. No raging here; just a search for quiet and for at least a few moments when life doesn't hurt so much . . .

The next time you reach for that tranquilliser or that drink, ask yourself whether it might not be good to meet the pain or loneliness head-on for a change . . . We have more resources than we usually think; we may never discover them and therefore never discover ourselves fully, if we do not enter the pain and suffering that tests our depths and tests them true.

There is a place in life for the experience of pain, not for its own sake, but because it burns the dross off . . . in a way that nothing else can . . . Those who never learn to live with pain only make themselves more vulnerable to it . . . They miss the self-identity that emerges when we truthfully confront the real challenges of living . . . People are ordinarily afraid that they will miss the meaning of life if they miss one of its possible pleasures; they run a far greater risk of missing its meaning when they shy away from its sufferings . . . so rage a little against the real suffering in your life . . .

Eugene C Kennedy

Not for ease? Why not?
What's wrong with ease?
For most of us the
Problem is not self indulgence,
But that we allow ourselves too little.
Prohibitions, counsels of perfection,
Drive us and load us up with guilt.

Time enough for courageous living
And all that rock-smiting.
Let's rest and wander in green pastures
When we find them, make the space
To let ourselves be loved;
Build up our strength
And grow in confidence;
Drink living water springing in
Great fountains;
Feed on the Bread of Life which
Satisfies.

Then we shall have provision
For the journey, and at last
Arrive, not too unpractised
In the art of resting
In his presence.

Ann Lewin

I call to you, O Lord, from my quiet darkness. Show me your
mercy and love. Let me see your face, hear your voice, touch
the hem of your cloak. I want to love you, be with you, speak to
you and simply stand in your presence. But I cannot make it
happen. Pressing my eyes against my hands is not praying, and
reading about your presence is not living in it.

But there is that moment in which you will come to me, as
you did to your fearful disciples, and say: 'Do not be afraid; it is
I.' Let that moment come soon, O Lord. And if you want to
delay it, then make me patient. Amen.

Henri Nouwen

STAYING WITH THE PAIN – IN CIRCUIT MINISTRY

Last week, according to the Lectionary, the Gospel passage was the one in Luke 14, which in the Good News Bible is entitled 'The Cost of Being a Disciple'. It is pretty stark and uncompromising - 'Whoever does not carry his own cross and come after me cannot be my disciple.'

I suppose I've always tended to relate 'bearing a cross' to the experience of imprisonment, torture, physical pain, and associated it with people like Bishop Leonard Wilson of Singapore, Martin Luther King, or Terry Waite, which makes it fairly remote from my humdrum existence. But maybe it also has something to do with keeping on, or staying put, when all you really want to do is run away.

As someone who is on the verge of retirement from the Methodist ministry, it seems to me as I look back, that the most exacting spell came in the wake of an invitation to follow a distinguished colleague so that he could take up a significant leadership role in the Church. Even the prospect of succeeding a minister with such an illustrious reputation was daunting. But I had more than twenty-five years' experience behind me, so I reckoned I knew a thing or two.

He sketched out a few ideas for me, and gave it as his opinion that it would be all to the good if I settled down for at least eight years because the church in question had experienced many changes of ministry in a relatively short space of time. He promised to brief me fully on every aspect of the work. But then he suffered a massive stroke, which sadly deprived the Church of a richly gifted leader, and me of my briefing.

However, after a few months in the appointment, it was too difficult to construct a strategy for the church's life, and for the first two years or more the work went well. Then things began to falter. Certain key figures moved away and were not replaced. Others died. The congregation was not growing. Evening worship was transferred from the church to a small chapel on the premises, and in due course it was decided to hold the evening service only once or twice a month. As some of the young people went on to higher education, and others moved, the Sunday Night Group ceased to meet. House Groups, after an encouraging beginning, petered out. The Sisterhood declined in numbers. Pastoral life was dominated by the response to substantial numbers of applicants for the baptism of their children, and although there was a careful and coherent policy for dealing with baptism – initiated by my predecessor – it was a source of some strain for the congregation.

Four mornings a week, and often into the afternoons as well, I would sit in the vestry, and all sorts of people would come in – church members or colleagues, but also people off the street with a wide range of needs. This was rewarding. But it was also time and energy-consuming, and it did not show up in terms of increasing the congregation, or the membership, or the Sunday collections - the traditional indicators of success!

I worked away at the preaching and the worship, did not let up on pastoral care, kept up with the administration. But I sensed the disappointment in the people that the church was not progressing. Was it me? What was I doing wrong? Should I go? But I had promised the Circuit (and my predecessor) to stay. I felt trapped. Somehow I had to hang on.

What sustained me? There was a core of fine, mature Christian women and men, utterly reliable, loving, imaginative, humorous – they are still there! There were my ministerial colleagues, varied in gender, race and theological emphasis, caring and mutually supportive. There was – and is! my wife, sharing everything, never faltering. And I said my prayers, and waited for the tide to turn. But it didn't.

In Luke 14, after declaring, 'Whoever does not carry his own cross and come after me cannot be my disciple', Jesus goes on to tell a story. It is about a man planning to build a tower. Jesus says that such a man should first sit down and calculate what it will cost, because if he runs out of money and can't finish the job, he will be a laughing-stock. And the story is intended as a warning to any would-be followers. They should pause to consider what they are letting themselves in for by becoming his disciples.

The cost of discipleship *has* been measured for some in imprisonment, torture, pain, even death. But in modern Britain discipleship – or ministry – is a matter of working away, often with small groups of people – 'the faithful remnant' – and seeing very little in terms of 'results'. That is how it is in this country. It is not like that in Africa, or the West Indies, or the United States. But the Church in Britain is hanging on by its eye-teeth. And simply keeping on and staying put is costly.

Anon

I sit by your side.
I have nothing to say.
There is nothing I can do.
I am anxious.
I am afraid.
But I stay.

Jim Cotter

Darkness shall
not frighten us
or distress wear
us out; we will
go on waiting,
watching and
praying until the
star rises.

Fr Alfred Delp

I see your hands,
not white and manicured,
but scarred and scratched and competent,
reach out –
not always to remove the weight I carry,
but to shift its balance, ease it, make it bearable.
Lord, if this is where you want me
I'm content.
No, not quite true. I wish it were.
All I can say, in honesty, is this:
If this is where I'm meant to be,
I'll stay. And try.
Just let me feel your hands.
And, Lord, for all who hurt today –
hurt more than me –
I ask for strength and that flicker of light,
the warmth, that says you're there.

Eddie Askew

As the dove gently settles on the tree,
receive the gift of peace.
As the flame rises free with light and warmth
receive the gift of life.
As the wind moves and dances round the earth,
receive the gracious gift of the Spirit.

Unsleeping friend
when I come to the end of my strength
and my work has no blessing in it
help me to remember you,
to reach for the hand of a friend
and find your love is there.

Bernard Thorogood

It's dark now –
And I'm flying low.
Cold.
But deep within me
I remember
A darkness like this
That came before.
And I remember

That after that hard dark –
That long dark –
Dawn broke.
And the sun rose
Again.
And that is what I must
Remember now.

Ken Walsh

17

CARING AT HOME

MOTHERCARE

Mother and child

I wonder what you are thinking as you sit there.
Are you remembering how you washed the
Child you bore? These hands, so
Frail and gnarled now, washed and
Gentled me. Now I wash you.
Your feet, so painful sometimes,
Carried you on endless journeys of caring;
Kneeling to wash them is an act of homage.
Are you remembering how, when you were young,
You pleased yourself about what you wore, and
Where you went? Now another puts your clothes ready,
And guides your unsteady steps.
Who is the child now, who the mother?
Do you remember sitting as I do,
Torn between wanting to help, and needing to
Leave dignity and independence free? Was it
A kind of death to you, that to be free,
I had to grow away? Your freedom now
Can only come through death, a
Painful letting go for both of us.

We'll never talk about these things,
But sometimes, when I tuck you into bed,
You look at me with impish humour,
As though you know what I am thinking,
Child, mother.

Still growing

My mother died some time ago.
The person I now care for,
Though she looks the same,
Has lost her power.
No longer archetypal,
Giver of life, solver of problems,
Source of wisdom, but
A frail old lady, confused and
Almost past the stage of knowing it.
(Though suddenly the other night
She said, 'Old age defeats me,
Who'd have thought that I'd go
Funny in the head like this?')

Watching her tears me inwardly.
Why should she suffer this disintegration,
Going on wearily from day to day?

Yet in her waiting there is hope.
Delightful still in personality,
She grows serenely on to her next stage.
Faltering strength and ceasing to be mother
Are staging posts, not ends, for her.
She's waiting in anticipation for her next
Adventure. 'When the time is right,' she says,
'I'll go.'

Day after day

The two poems printed just before this article describe some aspects of what it felt like during the eleven years or so when care for my mother dominated my life. Four years after the end of my stint of 'mother care', my chief memory is of the sheer relentlessness of the demand. For the last nine years of her life, my mother needed virtually full-time care, and when I wasn't providing it myself, I had to ensure that it was provided by someone else. There were a number of people who came in to be with mother during working hours, Monday to Friday. Sometimes the rota fell apart because the carers moved on, and there were some anxious times until replacements could be found. Out of working hours, one of my brothers, who actually lived with mother, bore a large share of the care, but there were always some things that he could not, or she would not have allowed him to do. Any decisions about what either my brother or I wanted to do, from staying late at work to going on holiday, had to be made within the context of mother's continuing need.

How long, O Lord, how long?
A silly question.

Do you, beyond the tick of time
For whom a thousand years
Flash like an evening,
Do you know how it feels
When evenings, days, months,
Drag, a thousand years?
The seeming endlessness of care,
Commitment carrying on
Long after energy is spent,
Do you, who slumber not,
Know that bone-weariness?

'My strength sufficient.' Yes,
I hear you, Lord. My head
Acknowledges that you are right.
The question in my guts is,
Is it true? Can I hang on
Until your timelessness
Pervades my life, and
Makes the question meaningless?

(De Profundis)

That was written eight years into caring for my mother in her increasing frailty and dementia. I didn't know then that there were still more than two years to go.

One of the hardest things was that there was no immediate end in view. Of course, ultimately there would be death, painful to contemplate, longed for yet dreaded. Many carers put a brave face on what is in fact a very painful situation – watching the disintegration of someone you love tears you apart inwardly. Some, perhaps many, carers find the thought crossing their mind that it's a pity that death cannot be hastened – it would be such a simple way out. When the life of the one you care for hangs by a thread anyway, it would be so easy to snap it. By the grace of God, most of us draw back from harming the person we care for because we feel that it would be a terrible betrayal of trust. But don't let's pretend that the issue doesn't arise.

Of course, it wasn't unremitting difficulty. There is satisfaction in caring for someone you love and making life as interesting and comfortable as possible. There was a lot of laughter, partly because laughing with mother dissipated some of her embarrassment about some of the situations she got herself into, partly because some things just were funny. There were activities she responded to which my brother and I enjoyed as well: trips in the car to the country, especially when there were new-born animals around; visits to stately homes and gardens, which were possible once she agreed to use a wheelchair. Hearing her talk about her childhood as a farmer's daughter was fascinating too. Long after those activities became impossible, she would always respond when I sang to her. We've always been a singing family, and hymns (even though we're not Methodists!) were a shared delight. They became my way of praying with and for her in the last year or so, when she was in a rest home, and I used to go in and settle her for the night.

The grace of God keeps us going, but not in any facile way. Believing in God, in my experience, doesn't solve problems. It raises some very big questions, not least about suffering. I don't believe God sends suffering – it is just part of the world we live in. I believe God finds suffering as abhorrent as we do, but can't intervene to remove it without upsetting the laws by which the universe is set to live. So God is left suffering with us, and we with God. That is the heart of compassion, *suffering with*. I found myself increasingly able to relate to a God who is that vulnerable. That sense of being in it with God gave me new resources. God might not be obviously omnipotent, able to 'put things right' in any simplistic way, but I believed God would be unendingly faithful as we struggled together to make sense of the pain.

It was important to me to keep 'normal life' going alongside the care. Most carers feel resentment at the curtailment of freedom. If the ways in which we as individuals find refreshment are denied us, the person cared for is going to suffer from our bitterness. Keeping up my own interests added to the exhaustion at one level, but provided life at another. It was hard work establishing a care pattern that allowed it, but it was infinitely worthwhile. There are many groups around for carers now. For some they are a lifeline, and I wouldn't deny their value, but when I was up to the ears in demands, I didn't want to share other people's. I wanted some freedom to develop my own inner space, and come back to the care more fulfilled, with more to give.

I needed someone to talk to about my fears and frustrations, someone who would allow me to stay with the hard questions, and not tell me that everything was in God's hands as though that solved the problem; or tell me that I would feel better tomorrow – I knew from experience that bad days could be followed by worse ones.

I needed, too, to know that there were people who understood the problems who were working to establish systems that would allow proper, appropriate care to be given without draining or exploiting those who gave it. I was looking after my mother before 'Care in the community' became a politically fashionable phrase – and I am under no illusion about its cost, both in emotional and financial terms. Unfortunately government underestimates both – the emotional cost is higher when the physical resources are not adequate.

Life doesn't stop for carers either. The time when elderly parents need care will coincide for many with major changes in the pattern of life. Some of these are physical, especially for women, some social, as children grow through adolescence and leave home; and working patterns change. I had many adjustments to make, and there wasn't much energy to spare – it wasn't even possible to be ill in peace.

Being a carer is a time of struggle: juggling with demands on time, nourishing one's own inner life, wrestling with huge theological questions, fighting bureaucracy to ensure that one gets adequate help . . . and it ends with bereavement which is no less real and painful because it is expected, in some sense longed for.

I pondered a great deal during those years on the image of death as new birth. The struggle to die seemed to be like the struggle to be born: a desire to be free from the imprisoning constraints of failing body and mind similar to the struggle to be free from the womb which cannot provide space for growth any longer. As I watched my mother grow towards death, it seemed to me that I was feeling the birth pangs of her new life. Life had come full circle: death a second birth. In that imagery lay great hope.

Ann Lewin

However raw your life
and however much pain you bear,
can you use this very raw material
to allow God to shape you,
not for ease, but for glory?

Jim Cotter

I came across something that would be with me throughout my life. Oppositions break or solidify a person. I determined they would solidify me. I wouldn't bear things; I would use them. As a radiant woman said, 'My cheeks have been slapped so much they are quite rosy.'

I Stanley Jones

> Listen to the language of your wounds.
> Do not pine away in the pain of them,
> but seek to live from the depths of them.
> Make the extent of your desolation
> the extent of your realm.
>
> *Jim Cotter*

It is important to be in touch with our sorrows, to recognise them, to honour them even. So often we imagine there is virtue in pretending they don't exist. We treat them as Victorian *grandes dames* treated the wayward son, dispatching him to the colonies so that he could be forgotten or ignored until he returned home reformed, rich and famous. There is reason for that, of course. Having him around is painful, not least to the family pride.

In the same way, living in the presence of our sorrows is always painful, and one of the bits of us that is hurt most of all is our pride. I hate to acknowledge that I cannot love my mother; that I despise my brother; that I have made a mess of my career and my marriage. How much more comfortable to my self-esteem to push all those feelings away, to pretend to myself that everything in the garden is lovely, that summer will last for ever.

Charles Elliott

CARING WITHIN A HOSPICE
and as a
BEREAVEMENT COUNSELLOR

The modern hospice movement has, over the last thirty years, helped to begin to alter perceptions about dying and death. Death remains the greatest taboo subject, but the media, and the vast amount of literature on the market open windows on to the great unknown we call death. We choose to look or not to look through the windows offered to us.

Too many people fear hospices. 'I couldn't visit my friend in the hospice'. 'Don't ever let me go into a hospice.' The fear is that one might be confronted by darkness, death, doom and gloom. The reality is that hospices are usually places of light and love, of living and laughter together with the sadness. For most patients admitted to a hospice there is much that is surprisingly comforting and uplifting. Even for a dying person there may be a lot of healing.

I remember very clearly arriving at our local hospice with my husband on a late November evening in the dark many years ago now. The entrance doors were open, and the light from within streamed into the outside darkness. Two members of staff were there to greet us. As I came in behind my husband it was as if my cloak of anxiety and fear dropped off me. Later when he was comfortable in bed he hugged himself and said, 'I feel so sheltered and safe.' For both patient and family hospice care can be full of immeasurable gifts, given by ordinary people in unobtrusive ways, and this can mean that people may know a lot of healing even though they may not be cured.

A lady came with advanced malignant disease, a year after her husband's death, and after years of a cruel marriage. She felt destroyed and looked a mess. The second day at the hospice she was being made comfortable in a chair, a rug around her knees and a drink put within reach. 'I have never felt I was worth anything in all my life,' she said, 'but here everyone makes me feel important.' The staff helped to improve her appearance, and she gradually realised she was respected and that people cared about her. Shortly before she died she said to me, 'I have reached a plane of life here that I couldn't imagine existed.' She died, but she was healed.

Perhaps, above all, hospice care whether it be in-patient care, day-care, or care in the community, takes away a surrounding atmosphere of fear. And patients who have been held on to by loving families feel a permission to let go. A patient who feels they have permission to die can find a peacefulness that is almost tangible.

I have talked about the patients. Hospice care also offers support and comfort to families and friends, and afterwards there is on-going support in their bereavement. So who gives the care? Who takes away some of the fear? Who shares the anxieties? How do the carers survive?

Any of us who choose to work in a hospice, who sit beside a terminally ill patient, who find ourselves caring for the dying as part of our job, who care for the bereaved as a counsellor, friend, neighbour or pastoral visitor find some satisfaction, however difficult the experience may be. Most of us, at some stage in life, will find ourselves nursing or visiting someone who is terminally ill but we do not have to be involved in a hospice or hospice care. We do not *have* to be a Cruse counsellor, or a pastoral visitor who visits those who have been bereaved. This is something we choose to do.

Over ten years I went to work every day in our local hospice and every day I felt it was a privilege to work there. I do not lose sight of the ordinary, everyday annoyances that are always there in any work situation, the times when it was very difficult to feel harmonious with a colleague, the patients who expressed huge anger, the families of patients who, because of anxiety, were critical and could never be pleased. A hospice is usually a small place with nowhere to hide, and yet often there was a huge amount where one took into oneself from other people and which one had to contain.

I hated hearing people say how 'dedicated' one was to work in a hospice. We were all ordinary people doing work we wanted to, feeling privileged in spite of all the natural feelings of inadequacy and helplessness one feels in the face of *not* being able to stop a person dying, of *not* being able to give the bereaved person the one thing they want.

Of course it is hard. All the time the rug is being pulled from under one's feet; hospice staff live with continual loss. There is often no time to stop and mourn. There is the next person, the next and the next. And too often as professionals we feel we need to 'cope' and to be 'strong'. Because so much is being taken from one, unconsciously one may grab at anything which gives false strength – 'I know things about this patient that no one else knows' – 'Her family told me things they couldn't tell anyone else.' And in all the business, communication becomes weak.

There are emotional and psychological pitfalls. So how do hospice staff survive? They survive because they love the work. To help someone have a 'good dying' is a wonderful gift to give, however small a part one plays. There is no dress-rehearsal for dying so it is very important to get it as right as one possibly can. To be with someone in their dying, or as they actually die is a profound experience. Death is *awesome*. There is so much unknown for us all, believer or non-believer. But here is an opportunity to catch a tiny bit of the future journey, to sense a transition we can only guess at. It *is* awe-inspiring. The most difficult part of the work for me was those times when I sat by someone in their dying who was full of fear. It required a great deal of courage sometimes to stay and acknowledge the fear, and share it as much as one was able to do so.

All the time there were the families and friends who watched and waited. They all had stories to tell, and secrets in their hearts they were prepared to share given time, privacy, a listening ear and heartfelt caring. To receive important confidences is like being given a precious gift to be held delicately as if it were a fragile piece of porcelain or a tiny new-born baby. People are generous in their sharing at important moments of their lives if someone will receive the sharing. The hospice staff are not usually the main givers but the main receivers of immeasurable gifts from those who come for care. Their courage, humour and thankfulness make one feel a deep sense of humility.

Very early in my years of hospice work I learnt – because I had to – that one must learn to be thankful for the little one can do, and must not feel guilty or destroyed by what one can't do. Of course we can never do 'enough'; and especially as Christians we may feel this.

The prayer of St Ignatius which extols us to 'give and not to count the cost; to fight and not to heed the wounds; to toil and not to seek for rest' leaves much to be desired. 'To labour and not ask for any reward save that of knowing that we do thy will' is a valiant prayer for Christians, though most of the time we have to go on in faith not knowing if we are doing God's will. But we *have* to 'count the cost' and to 'heed the wounds', and we must give ourselves rest. Jesus withdrew from the crowds to be by himself, to rest and replenish. So why must we deny ourselves? If we believe in loving our neighbour as ourself, how much do we love our neighbour if we spurn ourself? We cannot care for others if we do not care for ourselves.

There are skills to be learnt in order that we may sustain ourselves and our ability to do this work of caring for the dying and the bereaved. We have to learn to observe the boundaries of time and energy; to limit the length of a visit; to arrange another session but not to be on call all the time; to be able to say goodbye when the time comes. More difficult is to learn the inner boundaries, so that while one may share a person's pain one does not get sucked in and take responsibility for their anguish.

Certainly, if we choose to work with the dying and the bereaved we must consider our own needs. We can only stay beside the pain of others if we nurture ourselves. We need to find support within the organisation we work for; we need to find ways of discharging other people's burdens which we absorb; Above all we need to be able to replenish ourselves and our inner resources. For each of us the means will be different – friends, sport, music, poetry, being creative. By protecting ourselves we protect those for whom we care. If we allow ourselves to be assaulted by pain (continually) we become burnt out and desensitised.

Working with people who are bereaved is a constant being beside someone in pain. To go into the dark hole with a bereaved person, even for a short while, is a marvellous gift to give someone in the agony of bereavement. In darkness our eyes dilate to try and find some glimmer of light. In the same way the person in the blackness of grief will unconsciously reach out for any crumb of help or comfort. It is only when one returns from that place of desolation and darkness that one may realise the soul has reached out, grown and been touched as never before. Values have changed, unimportant worries have dropped away, God may be nearer than ever before. If we who help the bereaved can dare to share the darkness, we too will be changed.

As bereavement counsellors or friends of the bereaved we cannot bring the dead person back. We cannot make the situation all right. We cannot order joy to return. So how do we endure the feelings of helplessness and inadequacy?

We have to know humility, to know our own extreme frailty, to recognise how ordinary we are. We have to do so much caring work in trust and faith. We can never measure what we do. Occasionally someone will tell us that two years ago we said something helpful. We will not – we hope! – be told of the unhelpful things we have said and done.

For those who have a Christian faith there will be prayer to sustain and a belief that God is being a strength and an enabler. There are many people who would not call themselves Christians who are wonderful supporters and befrienders of the dying and bereaved. Perhaps we are all doing God's work but wear different labels.

We are all spiritual beings. We all, each in our own way, seek some sort of spiritual fulfilment. It seems to me that just as we practice a language we want to speak, a musical instrument we want to play, we need to practice our search for peace and contentment. So much we look for elsewhere, when all the time it is within ourselves. The deep centre of our beings can be the place where we find the strength and tranquillity to bear pain. While we are buffeted about on the surface of the ocean of life by wind and storm and scorching sun, deep, deep down at the bottom of the ocean is stillness, quiet and peace.

It is said that 'grief eats into you'. I have a vision of pain and grief and bereavement eating into us – it can be our own pain or the pain of others, making a bigger and bigger well inside us. Into that well can be poured bitterness, anger and loneliness. But with God's grace that well can be filled with loving, caring, compassion, understanding, the ability to reach out to others. At the very bottom of that well is our own place of grace and strength which cannot be sullied by the world, but which is there for us to get in touch with when we need to, even in the midst of a busy, noisy, pressing schedule.

We do not have to have degrees in knowing what to say or important qualifications in psychotherapy. We cannot on the whole *do* anything for the pain of the bereaved. We *can* offer ourselves, our presence, our respect, our faithfulness to their situation. It is not always easy; Sometimes it is difficult and demanding. Yet within us we can know that bereaved people can rediscover joy, and rejoin life. They will make the journey; we can only be beside them. That is a privilege and, in spite of all it demands, a replenishment in itself.

How can we do this? People say it must be so depressing. But I can say that it is not. My years at the hospice have transformed me and my life. I dare to say they were in some ways the most joyful of my life, because I was involved with people on such a deep level of unconditional caring and love.

All this work makes the heart unfold, and for me it brought new understanding and knowledge. It has given me a unique opportunity to make new discoveries about myself. It has helped me to work through fears, anger, huge self doubt, insecurities about relationships and life in general; and finally to come into contact with that space inside, deep down, which feels like unconditional love and caring.

Such love, when it enters your life, when you know it in yourself, turns into a deep contentment and serenity. So that mostly one *can* bear the pain of caring, and go on in faith and trust without any proof that one is good or clever or able. It is the well spring of wanting to reach out to another human being that is the never ending source of God within us.

Clarissa Robinson

* * * * *

We cannot name all the cross-bearers, but today remember those who have the long-term care of the sick in body and in mind, who often get tired and who may not be able to see a full recovery ahead.

> Spirit of endless compassion,
> your care for us
> is the support that all carers need,
> to transform weariness into patience,
> and patience into hope.
> Come, with strength and joy!

Bernard Thorogood

HEALING

What if pain does not go,
What then? Scars can be
Touched to raw response in
Unexpected moments
Long after the event which
Caused them, nerve ends twitch
Perhaps for ever after
Amputation.

Healing is not achieved
Without some cost. It
May not mean the end of
Pain. Healing can hurt
Just like fresh wounds,
As pockets of poison are
Lanced, or lesions cut to
Allow more flexibility. For
Healing is not going back
To what one was before,
It is a growing on
To a new stage of being,
Through many deaths and
Resurrections being set free.

Ann Lewin

When the discomfort has become so great that I can do nothing but lie down, and cannot think clearly, then I know my work has become prayer . . . This does seem a very churlish way to treat God . . . His humility appears endless . . .

It is very good to have something to try to do with the pain. While it remains an unmitigated evil, I can yet regard it somehow as a means to an end. I cannot describe the process very well, but I found it to be one of somehow *absorbing darkness* – a physical or mental suffering of my own or, worse, of someone else's into my own person, my own body or my own emotions. We have to allow ourselves to be open to pain. Yet all the while we must resist any temptation to assent to its being other than evil. If we are able to do this – to act, as it were, as blotting paper for pain, without handing it on in the form of bitterness or resentment or of hurt to others – then somehow in some incomprehensible miracle of grace, some at least of the darkness, may be turned to light.

Learning to live with the disorder as creatively as possible has in the end formed the person I am. I cannot, in the last resort, regret being the person I am.

Margaret Spufford

I have never read a poem extolling the virtues of pain, nor seen a statue erected in its honour, nor heard a hymn, dedicated to it . . . We seem to reserve our shiniest merit badges for those who have been healed, featuring them in magazine articles and TV specials, with the frequent side-effect of causing unhealed ones to feel as though God has passed them by. We make faith not an attitude of trust in something unseen, but a route to get something *seen* – something magical and stupendous, like a miracle or supernatural gift. Faith includes the supernatural, but it also includes daily, dependent trust in spite of results.

Philip Yancey

Companion, Comforter, Breath of life,
for those who have remained faithful
through long periods of pain
through years of disappointment,
through hard service in lonely places
We praise you Holy Spirit.

Bernard Thorogood

All this is known to him
And I am known to him
And his eternal peace is known to him –
I will sleep.

Sister Olga

CARING IN TIMES OF TRAUMA

Reflections of ordained men and women who have been involved in bearing the pain of those involved in major disasters.

It seems impertinent to write about my ministry, and I can only do it because I know it came from God, for more than at any other time in my life I felt God's constant presence with me.

I can't pretend that I have come through unscarred. I needed to tell my story but at first I couldn't tell my spouse – I think at that point I had to keep it out of the home.

Trauma needs to be shared freely before you can start to block things off, and with someone in whom you have total confidence. It has taken a long time for me to write about these experiences for unknown readers, and even as I write the tears flow down my face.

The pain and grief will heal but my life will never be the same. If tragedy such as this should strike again I would be there, but only if I felt that I was the right person to minister. I thank God for the privilege of sharing these people's lives.

* * * * *

Although I think I have come to terms with the trauma in which I was involved it has inevitably left a scar and a memory that can never be erased – nor would I wish it to be removed completely, as it has given me a greater compassion and a deep concern for a caring response by faith communities to the needs of others especially at times of acute trauma.

* * * * *

About the middle of the week that followed one of the counsellors asked, 'How on earth are you coping with all this?' I had never given it a thought. But when I did, I recalled that every night when I returned home there were several A4 sheets of telephone messages and many letters and cards – all saying

'We are thinking of you; we are praying for you', and I realised I was only the visible front of the care and compassion of the church and many other people. The prayers of many people and the presence of God was my support in a very tangible way.

* * * * *

Words spoken within a service shared by carers at a major disaster – they are relevant also to so much of our pain-bearing ministry.

We have shared a lot together this week. In our own ways we have been doing what we had to do and more. You will have been thanked and abused. There has been aggression, shouting and the level of noise during the first few days was at times almost unbearable. We have seen the worst side of human nature and also seen it at its best. We have all been crucified a little bit. Think of the better moments, the good, healthy, healing experiences and hang on to them. There is always the need for forgiveness in our dealings with each other.

> Inside,
> I am making myself strong.
> I am weaving bands of steel
> To bind my soul.
> I am knitting stitches of suffering
> Into my hands
> To make them strong.
> I am strengthening my mind
> With the warp and weft
> Of weariness and endurance.
> I am binding my faith
> With the bonds of psalms and songs
> Of all who have suffered.
> In time,
> I will be tempered like fine steel
> To bend, but not to break.
>
> *Margaret Pizer*

To preserve the silence within – amid all the noise. To remain open and quiet, a moist humus in the fertile darkness where the rain falls and the grain ripens – no matter how many tramp across the parade-ground in whirling dust under an arid sky . . .

Dag Hammarskjold

PRAYER IN CHRIST

Eternal Spirit,
Life-giver, Pain-bearer, Love-maker,
Source of all that is and that shall be.

With the bread we need for today,
feed us.
In the hurts we absorb from one another,
forgive us.
In times of temptation and test,
strengthen us.
From trials too great to endure,
spare us.
From the grip of all that is evil,
free us.

For you reign in the glory
of the power that is love,
now and for ever. Amen.

Jim Cotter

Our brokenness is the wound
through which the full power of God
can penetrate our being
and transfigure us in him.

Jean Vanier

CARRYING THE PAIN IN THE WORLD

I have always felt sorry for Atlas, the Titan who in Greek mythology was compelled by the gods to carry the whole universe on his shoulders. He is usually depicted as bent low under the sheer weight of the world resting on his back. It was an impossible burden for him to carry.

By contrast I enjoyed a cartoon that was drawn to publicise the Sixth Assembly of the World Council of Churches, which had as its theme 'Jesus Christ – the Life of the World'. The poster depicted a little man holding in his arms a giant globe. His face was wreathed in a smile, and his cheek rested affectionately on the earth's surface. Sad, suffering, sinful as that world might be, you felt that it was in the hands of one who loved it and for whom therefore the burden was light.

There are many people these days who find the burden of the world's suffering more than they can bear. The heart-rending pictures of famine-stricken children, the endless columns of refugees, the horrendous accounts of atrocities, the frustrated attempts at peace-making can lead us to total despair. We react either by switching off, quite literally if we have been watching the television news, or by succumbing to what has been called 'compassion fatigue'. We begin to feel so powerless to do anything that we become paralysed by guilt. Yet we are reminded right at the beginning of St John's gospel that we follow one who 'takes away the sin of the world' not by ignoring its pain and its wickedness, but by bearing in himself the cost of an all-embracing love.

Right at the heart of our gospel stands the assertion that 'God so *loved* the world', and we who love God dare not allow ourselves to stop loving this world even in all its suffering. Loving means bearing the pain of the beloved and doing all in one's power to relieve it, but it also means that the burden becomes light because love generates its own strength. There is wisdom in the old story of the lad who was carrying a toddler on his back.

When a passer-by sympathised with him for having to bear such a burden, he responded, 'That's no burden; that's my brother!' When we recognise the whole of humanity as our family, helping to carry their burdens becomes not just a duty but a privilege. We know that we are sharing not only in the fellowship of Christ's suffering but also in the power of his resurrection. For to the Christian the world is never a place to despair of; it is the arena of God's activity and the place where he is working out his purpose.

John Wesley once said, 'God looks on each soul as though it were a whole world, and on the whole world as though it were a single soul.' One of my favourite prayers is one of Michel Quoist's that asks for this kind of vision which is both personal and cosmic:

> I would like to rise very high, Lord,
> Above my city,
> Above the world,
> Above time.
> I would like to purify my glance and borrow your eyes.
> I would then see the universe, humanity, history, as the
>   Father sees them . . .
> Then falling on my knees, I would admire, Lord,
>   the mystery of this world
> Which, in spite of the innumerable and hateful snags
>   of sin,
> Is a long throb of love, towards love eternal.

When we are oppressed by a sense of the hopelessness of a world in which there is so much suffering, we ought not to turn our face away from it, but rather to look more closely into it in order to discern all the signs of love at work. They are there in every situation: the sheer courage and persistence of the human spirit, the self-sacrifice of those who put their own lives at peril for the sake of others, the agencies that are working for the values of the kingdom of heaven in the midst of the kingdoms of earth. All these need the reinforcement of our own resources of faith and hope and love.

I was made acutely aware of this a couple of years ago when I visited a refugee camp in Kenya, on the border of the Sudan. I admit that I dreaded going there. I had shrunk from seeing on television those long columns of homeless, helpless people trekking across the desert, fleeing the pursuing armies in the civil war that had so devastated their land. But meeting those people face to face was an extraordinary experience. Most of them were little more than schoolboys, many of them with legs blown off by the landmines scattered all over the territory. Yet here they were, with the help of aid workers and the United Nations' refugee services, remaking their lives in home-made tents in a foreign land, even playing football with their crutches! With them, keeping up their spirit quite literally, was a young Sudanese Catholic priest who had kept them going all through their long trek through the desert by gathering them together daily for prayer and for spiritual 'reinforcement' as he called it.

We need that kind of faith in the resourceful power of prayer. Too often we seem to regard intercession as a kind of off-loading of our responsibilities on to God's shoulders. We list before the Lord a whole catalogue of troubled areas of the world, scarcely pausing to hear what he might have to say about those situations to us. But if we believe that prayer acts as a kind of trigger, prompting us to action, then maybe we should take our intercessions more slowly and more sparingly. If we concentrate the energy of our thought upon one or two particular situations we may well find ourselves called to some active response.

I remember clearly a day almost thirty years ago when the world woke up to the news that Russian tanks had invaded Prague, bringing to an end the brief Springtime of hope the Czechs had enjoyed under the leadership of Dubcek. In a service I attended that morning, the person leading the intercessions invited us not simply to pray for but to feel with those people whose own personal lives would have been shattered by this political tragedy. Immediately there came into my mind a Czech woman I had met only the day before, enjoying her first holiday in England. I thought of what the news on the radio must have meant for her. I felt compelled to go and seek her out to give whatever help I could in enabling her to return home. That was the beginning not only of a lifelong friendship but of a continuing concern about subsequent events in what is now the Czech Republic. It was also a warning that when we pray sympathetically, God may require us to turn that sympathy into practical support.

It may not always be support of such a personal kind as I have described. Indeed there is a danger at times of wanting to be so personal in the aid we give that we ignore the larger issues of the causes of the world's hunger and poverty and pain. When I worked for the Overseas Division of the Church I was often tempted to come home from a visit abroad and plead the case of some child whose plight had particularly moved me and who I knew could be helped if only some generous donor might be found to supply her needs. But then, what of all the other children whose needs were equally clamant? And what of the school struggling to cater for the children on a budget so meagre that they could not even pay the fees of the teachers? And what of the Church officials trying to balance one need against another as they drew up their budget? And what of the national government facing cuts in its expenditure on education because of the need to pay off its debts for aid given in the past? I soon realised that to take seriously the pain of the world means to be caught up in a whole network of conflicting claims. Gradually I came to the conclusion that such aid as I could give must, like the love of God, be undiscriminating and all-embracing. It must involve not only personal giving but social action and political awareness which could well demand more of me than the mere opening of my purse.

When we do start tackling such world issues we can begin to feel powerless, as though we are up against powers and principalities far beyond our comprehension. Anyone who has attempted to confront those who are powerful in this world with the evil effects of their power knows how complex such encounters can become. During the days of the anti-apartheid campaigns I recall how we sought interviews with the heads of large corporations who were known to have big stakes in South Africa that were bolstering the apartheid regime. We used to feel then like Davids confronting Goliaths, though without any stones in our sling! Yet when we met those whom we thought to be giants, their power so often seemed to be elusive or evasive. We ourselves were sustained by the realisation that the only power that can truly transform the world is God's power. Prayer is the means of helping to release that power into the world. Charles Elliott in his book *Praying the Kingdom* describes such prayer as 'adding one's own soul-force to the cosmic struggle of the love of God against the powers of darkness'. Then in the awareness of God's power we lose the sense of our own powerlessness.

There is enough evidence in the world's history of the eventual triumph of that love of God to keep us going even when it seems as though we hope against hope. The abolition of slavery, the granting of universal suffrage and, in our own time, the overcoming of apartheid are but three illustrations of ways in which active commitment can bring about change. All such movements have relied on the obedience of people who, having seen a vision of what could be, resolved to set about changing things as they were. We cannot all be involved in every issue but we can each be committed in some way to helping to relieve the world's burden of pain and in working to overcome the evil that causes so much of it.

As I write this article our news programmes are dominated by pictures of the shelling and bombing in Bosnia. Prayers for Bosnia have become a regular part of the litany of intercession in most churches these days. Whenever we pray for peace I find myself questioning what I personally can do about the suffering caused by war. I almost envy those who have the courage and the resources to go out themselves to take humanitarian aid to the war zones. But I know that even more vital is the need for the fighting to end. I pray for the peace-makers but what of the arms manufacturers? They need our prayers too – the prayer Jesus prayed for those who crucified him: 'Father, forgive them, for they know not what they do.' But the evil that they do needs to be exposed and resisted in his name. So I share in the Campaign Against the Arms Trade and dare to believe that one day the prophecies will indeed come true and people will convert the weapons of war into the instruments of peace.

Perhaps the hardest thing of all to bear is our own part in causing the suffering in the world. We know all too well that we benefit from the global injustice, that we are the fortunate, the powerful, the privileged ones. That very sense of guilt could paralyse us. On the other hand, it could become the galvanising force generating in us the energy to strive against the injustice and to do what we can to alleviate its effects. For we too are forgiven. The Lamb of God who takes away the sin of the world takes away our sin too. He sets us free to go out into the world with good news. This is the world God loves. Therefore we can love it too and, in the strength of his love, carry our share of its burden.

. *Pauline Webb*

You are the needy one.
You are in my power.
I can refuse to be with you.
I can reject you within myself.
Or I can be with you,
loving you,
gently touching you.
You challenge me to a choice.
You judge me.

Jim Cotter

In the pain, misfortune, oppression,
and death of the people,

God is silent.
God is silent on the cross,
in the crucified.
And this silence is God's word,
God's cry.
In solidarity,
God speaks the language of love.

Jon Sobrino

I believe, although everything
hides you from my faith.
I believe, although everything shouts No! to me . . .
I believe, although everything may seem to die.
I believe, although I no longer would wish to live,
because I have founded my life
on a sincere word,
on the word of a Friend,
on the word of God.

I believe, although I feel alone in pain.
I believe, although I see people hating.
I believe, although I see children weep,
because I have learnt with certainty
that he comes to meet us
in the hardest hours,
with his love and his light.
I believe, but increase my faith.

From Livro de Cantos
(Porte Alegre, Brazil)

There is a tendency in all of us to collapse after trying events and feel sorry for ourselves. This is when people prone to migraines get them, when nervous exhaustion is experienced and when ulcers appear. So there should be no surprise when this occurs. The question is: do we just treat the symptoms when they occur, or are there spiritual principles which might prevent this happening?

In Elijah's case, God provided direct sustenance and encouragement while he was still alone. But more often comfort comes from a good friend who can pull us out of our slough of despair and self-concern and lift our eyes to the wider world around us and God's purposes for the next stage of our life. For the apostle Paul, Titus was such a friend, a younger man whose growth and development as a Christian he owed to Paul. Titus also found his opportunity for ministry by assisting Paul in his travels and in founding churches.

This is so often the way it works for us. I have found this to be true over thirty years of pressurised ministry, especially in social welfare and refugee work, where you feel the great weight of responsibility of supporting staff and at the same time identifying with the terrible problems of homelessness, abuse and human rights violations that people suffer. Friends are the best antidote against feeling weighed down and lonely.

Many friends are better than one friend. As Paul found, Demas, on whom he had relied in establishing one of the New Testament churches, had 'deserted' him and he had to call on other friends to fill the gap. He was lucky: Luke the doctor and other friends quickly stepped in.

Some Christians worry that surrounding yourself with friends prevents you from ever finding those quiet moments with God. But it does not have to be like that. You can see from the life of Jesus that sometimes he wanted his disciples around him, and even great crowds, but there were other times he badly wanted to be alone with his heavenly Father, and people were getting in the way. Neither is better than the other; different times call for different approaches. But whatever happens, it is better not to be utterly alone. Everyone needs friends.

David L Fleming

Moving away is only to the boundaries
of the self. Better to stay here,
I said, leaving the horizons
clear. The best journey to make
is inward. It is the interior
that calls. Eliot heard it.
Wordsworth turned from the great hills
of the north to the precipice
of his own mind, and let himself
down for the poetry stranded
on the bare ledges.
For some
it is all darkness; for me, too,
it is dark. But there are hands
there I can take, voices to hear
solider than the echoes
without. And sometimes a strange light
shines, purer than the moon,
casting no shadow, that is
the halo upon the bones
of the pioneers who died for truth.

R S Thomas

The world has kissed my soul with its pain, asking for its return in songs.

Rabindranath Tagore

'EVERYONE HAS THEIR OWN BURDEN TO BEAR'
Galatians 6:5

In normal circumstances 'bearing our own burden' is about coping with all it means to be human beings, people who make mistakes, who become ill, who are hurt, who are caught up in situations which make us feel helpless. And so often the 'burden' we carry appears to be a consequence of circumstances beyond our control – our upbringing, our personality, our temperament, our situation at work, our relationships at home, other people's attitudes towards us, our own insecurity . . . or any of the myriad happenings which impinge on our lives and bring us hurt or pain.

Even the responsibilities and challenges that ordinary day-to-day living brings can, in certain circumstances, bring too great a pressure to bear on us or inflict too deep a level of hurt, so that we begin to feel everything is too much for us and that life is not being fair. Whether we like it or not, however, 'bearing our own burden' is ultimately our responsibility and however much we share our pain or are able to rely on the love and support of family and friends we are, in the final analysis, alone in our individual uniqueness and experiences and inner thoughts and feelings, and we have to come to terms with life as it is and with ourselves as we are.

At the moment of writing I am finding this a difficult subject to approach. Yesterday I sat in the hospital waiting room while my husband had an injection into the nerves around a disc in his spine in the first stage of two possible further surgical processes to relieve him of the constant pain induced by a bad car crash five years ago. Today I have just made my daily visit to a close friend who is terminally ill. Both situations bring their own tension. Moreover my accompanying frustration of feeling helpless to do anything other than give practical help where possible is compounded by having spent the last few years caring for my much loved mother until her death.

There is tiredness, too; the tiredness common to all of us who refuse to recognise our limitations and expect too much of ourselves in terms of work! And there is an inner sadness difficult to put into words but due mainly to the fact that during the year I have found myself forced to accept many more far-reaching changes in life than I find easy to manage. So, as I feel at the present, it would have been much easier to ask someone else to share their thoughts than to try to get in touch with my own 'burden' in this rather public way. On the other hand I am writing out of a learning experience and in spite of the apparent catalogue of woes in the previous sentences I have found much that is positive and creative even within the most pain-filled moments of what has not been an easy period.

If, with the heading in mind, I concentrate now on ways that I have found help me to 'carry my own burden', it will not be to deny for a moment the strength I have received from family and friends and from all kinds of unexpected moments and comments. But no-one else can live our life for us and we all know, anyway, that at times our 'distress-signals' are not noticed or are, for one reason or another, apparently ignored and then we are indeed thrown back on our own resources and it is inevitable that this should be so. We are all 'pain-bearers' on our own behalf as well as being 'pain-bearers' on behalf of others; and it is often the case that those on whom we would most naturally rely are themselves struggling to cope with more problems of their own than we are aware.

It would be easy and all too glib to say that I find my strength depends on the love and presence of God in such times. I do actually believe this to be the case but I would have to admit that it is rarely something of which I am conscious when the going is hard. In fact I am more conscious of what seems to be God's absence than his presence and it is only in retrospect that I am aware of the strength or comfort I have received, or of the underlying sense of gentle support that has made life possible. I think for me this is the essence of faith – to trust that God truly is there for me and to know that whatever I feel or don't feel I have proved in the past that he has been deeply present in all I have experienced.

And so I have begun to learn how to rest in that assurance and how to allow God's grace to be available for me. The discipline and pleasure of worship, the increasing blessing of natural beauty – and of flowers and trees in particular – the courage to say 'for now I can do no more', an hour or so of quietness, allowing music to release my tears – these all become 'strength-bearers' for me. They don't take away the grief or the hurt or the tiredness or fear or whatever it may be that is weighing me down but they do somehow draw me into a world beyond my own personal horizons and remind me of all the loveliness and promise which is there for my refreshment and renewal.

I have also begun to learn to rely much more heavily on 'the sacrament of the present moment' – not just trying to live a day at a time, though that in itself is vital – but trying consciously to look for the little blessings along the way – a smile in the supermarket, a relaxing programme on television, a shared meal, a journey without a traffic jam! – all these remind me that there really are always blessings to count. As the friend I mentioned, who is so ill, said to me the other evening, 'I take Elizabeth Jennings' advice every night before I go to sleep and

> "Count the moments of my mercies up,
> I make a list of love and find it full.
> Others examine consciences. I tell
> My beads of gracious moments shining still."'

Over the years I have discovered a great deal about the necessity of 'letting go' and of 'acceptance'. After my father's death when I was eight years old, I went to five different schools in two and a half years and, for many years my mother and I seemed always dependent on other people's charity. Then when I was fifteen she had to spend several months in hospital which meant I had to 'board' at the local school – in itself a learning experience! All these experiences, though, in what was in so many ways a very happy childhood, taught me a good deal about finding resources within myself with which to respond to circumstances beyond my control – and they were not always positive ones! At the age of eleven, having had a rough time as a newcomer at several schools I decided I would be the one to 'bully' and be on top! Fortunately I don't think this stage lasted long! – but I am still aware that what other people often see as a 'reserve' or 'defensiveness' in my attitude (and which is not how I perceive my behaviour at all!) is almost certainly a legacy from those earlier years when I was at times excruciatingly aware of my 'aloneness'. So it has taught me to be very wary of making adverse judgments about other people's apparent attitudes and responses. I am firmly convinced that underneath we all have our own reasons for insecurity and for finding certain 'burdens' harder to bear than others.

Another kind of 'pain' we are nearly all called upon to bear at some stage in our lives is physical pain or disability which threatens our well-being and reminds us of our inevitable mortality. Fortunately in recent years I have not had the health problems which beset me in my twenties and early thirties but I did then on two occasions know that I might not recover from particular illnesses, and shall not easily forget the feeling of unreality when I lived with the knowledge that my blood count was giving clear indications that I had leukaemia; or the occasion when a pelvic abcess after major surgery reduced me to five-and-a-half stones in weight. Both experiences were clearly burdens to be borne but from them I learnt the very clear and reassuring truth – for me at any rate – that when one is very ill one's perspective on death is very different from the perspective you imagine it will be when you are bursting with health. In weakness of that kind I believe we do indeed discover strength. Editing the *Thorns In The Flesh* series has reinforced for me again and again this belief that in adversity of any kind people do discover within themselves a strength and ability to bear both pain and the unknown in a way they would never have imagined possible.

But for me, as for many of us I guess, a much harder load to have to bear is in watching members of my family suffer continual ill health or ongoing pain or to watch them struggle with unemployment or the threat of it. Others have written about the suffering this involves for the carer or the family member and I, with them know all too well that to have to, as it were, watch from the sideline is not an easy position to be in. Not so easy to admit to, perhaps, is one of the underlying pains we have to bear in such situations, the pain of having to live with the limitations that other people's disability or illness imposes on us. We can no longer do the things together that we would like to, we are circumscribed in activities and relationships and again, it is about 'letting go' not just for ourselves but for other people's sake and because we have no choice in the matter; to 'let go' in this way and to do it gladly is easier to write about than to achieve!

In her book *Living With Contradictions*, Esther de Waal writes 'No-one can be a good host who is not at home in his own house. Nor can I be a good host until I am rooted in my own centre. Then, and only then, have I something to give to others.' I see this as being profoundly true in relation to the way in which being able to bear our own pain enables us more fruitfully to bear the pain of others. It is a fundamental necessity in counselling that those who counsel must be able, as far as is possible, first to come to terms with their own pain and hurt before they try to alleviate the pain of others. So to be able to a large extent to 'bear our own load' is essential for those of us who seek to care for others in the name of Christ.

We need to try to understand ourselves, to accept ourselves with all our good and bad characteristics and motives, to acknowledge our own need and to be aware of our own limits. We need to be open to God's grace in all situations and trusting enough to receive, as Jesus said 'what will be given us in that hour'. And we need to be encouraged by the fact that there is overwhelming Christian testimony that what might in anticipation seem unbearable is usually found to be not only a 'burden' that *can* be carried but also a load that is lighter than we expected because we find we are never carrying it on our own.

I am very aware that much of this exploration of the verse from Galatians may have seemed too personal, too introspective and for that I apologise. And yet it is only experience that has been burdensome for me that I can share with authenticity and even then it will not take much imagination to recognise that I have been selective in my sharing. We all carry deep within ourselves pain and failures and sadness that we can scarcely articulate let alone express to others. But so too are there hidden depths of joy and gratitude and loving wonder – the pain and the joy so closely interwoven that together they make us who we are and nurture us into growth and maturity and an ever-increasing awareness that we cannot bear anything on our own. Our total dependency is on the God who made us and who loves us and who bore his own burden of pain and rejection with courage and in faith.

I don't think any of us will ever find 'pain-bearing' other than costly. Simply to be stoical and pretend nothing is amiss for us is never going to be the perfect solution. Yet neither is it any use if we allow ourselves to spend our lives feeling hard done by and misunderstood. Instead we need to try to find the kind of balance that women in India demonstrate as they walk with ease whilst carrying what seem to us impossible burdens on their heads. It is the kind of balance beautifully expressed in the following prayer written by Lesslie Newbiggin –

> 'Give me, Lord, a stout heart to bear my own
> burdens, a tender heart to bear the burdens
> of others, and a believing heart to lay all my
> burdens on you, for you care for us.'

If, through God's grace, we can make this prayer our own and live accordingly, we open up the possibility of bearing even the heaviest burden in a spirit of trust and with renewed hope.

Ann Bird

Lord,
it is hard for us
to see your love
in the places of our tragedy, pain and grief.
It is hard to believe
that your love is greater than our evil.
Just give us grace
to keep looking
and believing
in the most impossible circumstances
and, as we do what little we can,
keep giving us the vision
of the height, depth, length and breadth
until we do see
and cannot help believing,
and our love, refined by yours,
rises above
sorrow, fear, guilt and shame
and we shine, your light
for good and bad alike,
through cross to resurrection,
with Jesus Christ our Lord.

Alan Gaunt

PRAYING FOR OURSELVES

Response: Healing Spirit, set us free.
From wearisome pain . . .
From the sharp sword of agony . . .
From burdens too great to bear in love for others . . .
From guilt and regret about times past . . .
From fearful memories and fear for the future . . .
From the depths of despair . . .

Response: Spirit of God, heal us.
Through the ministry of listening and of presence . . .
Through the bearing of one another's burdens . . .
Through the ministry of counselling and therapy . . .
Through the ministry of prayer and sacrament . . .
Through our expectant hearts and open minds . . .
Through the bringing of our wills into harmony with your
    loving purpose . . .
Through our joy in being the friends of God . . .

Jim Cotter

We have all experienced the bond of belonging. We have all known the feelings. We believed the promises, we danced at weddings, we cried for joy at a new baby's birth. We were secure in the feeling of being at home. But then the bond slips away from us so quietly that we don't even realise that we've lost the connection. Or we suddenly wake up to the fact that we've broken with the past, and we have no confidence in the future. We know too much of Judas, because we know too much of our own desperate urgings and darkest fears. We're afraid when we get too close to the failure of any relationship. We keep our distance. Like the impulse to retreat from a good friend who ends a marriage we had a stake in, we fear it could happen to us.

But in our shared likeness there is also something compelling about Judas. If there is a way back for him, then perhaps there is for us as well – not in retracing our past, but in discovering the love that comes to us from our future.

Ray S Anderson

There are so many kinds of cross to be carried that we never know what to expect.

Christ, who walked the way of the cross,
may each disciple be given strength to endure.

We do not know the price that others pay as they seek to follow Jesus, for you can't explain heartache or evaluate betrayal.

Whatever the calling may be:
to endure disability
to outlast disappointment
to carry frightening responsibility,
to be steadfast amid corruption,
may each disciple be given strength
to carry the cross with confidence and hope
and find you walking alongside.

O God, who did not take away from Jesus the cup of suffering, but in Jesus drank it to the end, enable your servants to carry whatever is needed to show your love and justice in the broken life of the world. Amen.

Bernard Thorogood

Spirit of God be
within me to strengthen me,
beyond me to draw me,
over me to shelter me,
beneath me to support me,
before me to guide me,
behind me to steady me,
round about me to secure me.

Jim Cotter

Tears

Thank God for tears,
the tears that flow unchecked,
that run in rivulets
down to the sea of God;
that have to merge eventually
with something larger than the self.

Thank God for tears,
the tears that bring release
for knotted nerves
twisted as sinews,
bringing a breathing out
beyond despair.

Thank God for tears,
and then beyond the tears,
beyond the hopelessness
that has to offer up the grief
till no more fall,
because no more can fall –

the tiny step that is a journey's start,
a slow step onward,
numb at first and seemingly dead,
where haltingly, but gradually
one grassblade starts to grow
watered by tears;
somehow a kind of healing can begin.

Cecily Taylor

And a woman spoke, saying, Tell us of Pain,
    And he said:
    Your pain is the breaking of the shell that encloses your understanding.
    Even as the stone of fruit must break, that its heart may stand in the sun, so must you know pain.
    And could you keep your heart in wonder at the daily miracles of your life, your pain would not seem less wondrous than your joy;
    And you would accept the seasons of your heart, even as you have always accepted the seasons that pass over your fields.

And you would watch with serenity through the winters of your grief.

Much of your pain is self-chosen.

It is the bitter potion by which the physician within you heals your sick self.

Therefore trust the physician and drink his remedy in silence and tranquillity:

For his hand, though heavy and hard, is guided by the tender hand of the Unseen.

And the cup he brings, though it burns your lips, has been fashioned of the clay which the Potter has moistened with his own sacred tears.

Kahlil Gibran

Lord, we pray for those who know intense suffering:
for those who groan with hunger
for those whose bodies are racked with pain through illness
for those who ache with loneliness
for those whose bodies are tired out with hard work
for those whose spirits are numbed by constant denial of their
    humanity
for those whose will is exhausted through failure
for those who know crushing sorrow.

Lord, you have the clear, sparkling water of life within you; and you share humanity's experience of shed blood; we pray for all who suffer, that they may know your solidarity in the intensity of their pain, and also receive the advocacy of the Holy Spirit to comfort and uplift them. Help them to find a faith that protects their inmost self from destruction; to experience the love and peace of God which no suffering can shut out if our faith keeps us open to you: to find an assurance of spiritual life which is renewed in vigour each day. We also pray that in our human mortality they may find hope of salvation as it is received in bread, healing, companionship, rest for body and mind, affirmation for the person they are, real achievement and meaningful goals, and joy, fresh each morning. And for those who will not find relief in this life we pray that you will impart courage and faith that their life was not lived in vain. Through Jesus Christ our Lord. Amen.

Denis Vernon

THE VICARIOUS GOD
(Some theological reflections on pain-bearing)

C S Lewis's doctor once stated that pain provides an opportunity for heroism, concluding that the opportunity is seized with surprising frequency. Perhaps what this is saying is that pain as a physical and mental aberration calls for a response – at one extreme despondency and despair, at the other courage and heroic fortitude.

The causes and circumstances of pain have to be taken into account when virtue is associated with it. What Dickens' character Martin Chuzzlewit sees as desolating blows of fate, Mark Tapley sees as opportunities 'for coming out strong'. I mean that there seems to me to be a significant difference between the pain and suffering that comes through deliberately exposing oneself to conflict and that which comes as, say, part of the natural process of growing older.

If there is to be an adequate Christian theology of pain and suffering, it must have within it some view about pain-bearing. Some of the world's religions approach suffering with passivity and acquiescence, others actively find a redemptive way or, in some cases discover its didactic role. There is a strand of Christian theology which interprets the origin of suffering in a particular form of cause and effect. Take the incident of the encounter between Jesus and the blind man (John 9). Here the existential question is raised, 'Teacher, whose sin caused him to be born blind? Was it his own or his parents' sin?' (John 9:2). Still today we find it difficult to accept imperfection and disability without question. It is even harder to square them with the concept of a loving and caring God.

Disability presumes a notion of ability, imperfection a notion of perfection, wholeness. Why do the innocent have to suffer? Why is one called to be a pain-bearer and another to live a fairly painless life? Society does not readily ascribe sin as the cause of suffering and disability. True, for example, there is a body of opinion that considers the plague of AIDS a punishment from God for the sin of homosexuality. There is a kind of God who smites his children with affliction. The testing of Job was to see whether he would curse the very ground of his being when he was touched by affliction.

But there are still those who, with Job, find it hard to charge God with unreason and yet Job has to ask the question eventually. When Job experiences running sores from head to foot, he breaks his silence against God and curses the day of his birth:

> Why should the sufferer be born to see the light?
> Why is life given to men who find it so bitter?
>
> (Job 3:20)

Bearing physical ailments, we are told, depends on the threshold of pain which differs from person to person. The pain of extreme toothache, for example, is a different kind of pain from the pain of someone feeling excluded or discriminated against. Mothers experience pain in giving birth which no male can experience in the same way. Yet we can understand imperfection in terms of inherited genetic characteristics. Genetic engineering may one day remove the need for certain kinds of pain-bearing. Experimenting with drugs may alleviate a lot of the physical pain-bearing. We may reach a point where analgesia is almost a permanent state. The pain of living in this 'vale of tears' (or is it now 'the city of tears'?) may be increasingly to do with the emotive and cognitive rather than the physical. In other words longevity may produce the symptoms of chronic boredom and purposelessness when the aches and pains of arthritis and other geriatric complaints have been minimised.

But what about the pain and distress of nations? The holocaust has raised the ultimate question in modern times put this way: 'Where was God in Auschwitz?' Alongside it is another question, equally hard to answer, as the Chief Rabbi, Dr Jonathan Sacks, has highlighted: 'Where is humanity in Auschwitz?' We now know there are no limits to bestiality and atrocity. Pain can be inflicted from one human being to another even to the point of extinction and finality. The long-range weapon, the laser and the like saves us from hearing the pain of mutilation and dying. So too, in Bosnia, it is plain to see the pain heaped by one tradition on another – xenophobia, greed, lust for power, insecurity and revenge bring blood in their wake. But even in such a painful situation, there are human beings who intervene, who bring help, who risk the process of mediation. There are those who take the pain of cross-fire, the bullet and the shrapnel, the false accusation. There are those who become entirely vulnerable in no-man's land.

Returning to the question about the blind man – Jesus does not provide an easy answer about obvious suffering. He does not confirm the hereditary view concerning the cause of disease, nor does he provide an alternative. Instead he stresses the opportunity that suffering provides to show the possibility of its overcoming, to highlight the possibility of transcendence through God's intervention. While Jesus is in the world, works of healing illustrate the presence of what he calls light. When night comes, and the light has gone, this work cannot go on. In our time, the night has not yet come. Miracles still happen where the light prevails.

Yet Jesus the healer is himself subject to pain. This comes through intervention in areas of conflict, through mediation, through the offering of a cheek to be slapped, a shoulder to carry a burden. There is that pain which emerges from the task of seeking and saving that which is being lost. This kind of pain is part of the redemptive process. It is the pain of agape seeking to love in total disregard of its own safety and well-being. In this sense it is far removed from the pain of self-indulgence and self-gratification.

The discomfort that comes through self-denial, through being a cross-carrying disciple following the imperatives of the gospel, is a far cry from the kind that comes through self-indulgence and self-pity. We all want to recognize, with Abraham Maslow, that there is a hierarchy of needs which have to be met, but this is a far cry from the transcendent demands of the gospel which call for self-abandonment, for giving and not counting the cost, for losing one's life in order to find it.

Bishop Desmond Tutu reminds us that 'a Church that does not suffer cannot be the Church of Jesus Christ'. There is an inevitable pain which comes from being followers of Christ in the world. And this is true of histories of nations and peoples seeking emancipation and redemption, as well as for individuals seeking their personal salvation. Tutu, like Bonhoeffer and Luther King, witnessed the suffering that comes from the interface between good and evil, between light and darkness. Such situations call for painful heroism.

Within life events pain can come unexpectedly. Its origin may lie in some rogue growth, some abnormality; it may come to the surface after years of dormant festering; it may lie deep in the subconscious or express itself psychosomatically out of some intractable relationship where unresolved and unreconciled forces are at work.

There is that treatment of pain which is seen as simply an aspect of the brain. In neuro linguistic programming, the therapist is taught to help the patient to construe pain in a visual way. Pain management consists in changing the dimensions of pain, its shape, colour and size. But this kind of pain can easily be dismissed as ephemeral, some sort of figment of the imagination proceeding from 'the heat-oppressed brain', easily dealt with by psychotherapy (or aspirin). A local analgesic is all that is called for.

Wherever pain comes from it has to be 'suffered', borne for a shorter or longer time. There is a pain which comes just from being human. There is no way of running away from this pain without running away from yourself. Some pain does indeed last a lifetime – the pain of separation at childbirth or the loss of homeland for the refugee. Separation for a couple after, say twenty-eight years of marriage can be the lancing of accumulated pain which has come through mistrust, deceit and inability to communicate. This can often lead to a new kind of pain-bearing.

Yet people's response to pain varies enormously. Some respond with heroic fortitude, others crumble under the sheer injustice and ignominy of being struck down out of the blue. In recent years two of my close colleagues from theological college days have died of cancer in their fifties. I witnessed their last days; one thrown into convulsion by a brain tumour, the other crippled by secondary cancer. Both showed me amazing heroism. Not the kind that placards itself. There are those, like Roy Castle, who show the kind of heroism which trumpets the faith of the sufferer. The pain such people bear is evident, just as is their faith and fortitude. They are written large for all to see and marvel at. My friends bore their final pain to a handful of people. But they too bore it as Christians, not asking 'why me?', not cursing the dying of the light, but holding the hand tightly, as holding the hand of God.

> One more hug
> One locking of the hands,
> One further stare,
> Signals all to let you know
> We're here, here for you,
> Even when the tubes are taken out
> And the bell summons visitors
> To leave.

We all have 'thorns in the flesh' to carry, as St Paul did. Some bear in their bodies the scars of living a Christ-like life of service. Paul reckoned he bore the marks of Jesus branded on his body (Galatians 6:17). Such thorns in the flesh are hard to remove. The marks of redemptive service to others are the stigmata of Jesus. Self-sacrificial service is always vicarious. There is that kind of pain which is both undeserved and vicarious. It is borne willingly on behalf of others both seen and unseen. We are to bear one another's burdens and by so doing fulfil the law of Christ (Galatians 6:2).

I had to address the desolate companions of a student who hung himself after failing his assignment. He chose a place deep in the woods to express a violent response to his emotional pain, a response that produced even more pain. His family, his friends, his tutor, those who discovered him still bear the scars. One way I dealt with the tragic event was to write a poem which I communicated to the campus and community.

Farewell to an Art Student

Why this place deep within the ancient wood
Where squirrels chase their tails?
These blood-red leaves have lately understood;
The sun descends – blanches, pales,
Brush strokes added to a dying day.
His life now fixed in our collective brain,
More rigid than the still trees,
Pastiche of him we'll never see again,
Portrait with a black-trimmed frieze,
Hung in the archives of our memory.

Yes, him we failed, much more than he failed
Failed to see the lines he sketched
Across the page – faint, blurred and colourless.
His life undrawn, untimely stretched,
Suspended in our hearts and minds.
But here within this place we sketch once more
The outline of a day ahead,
We pass along the cup of grief and store
The residual tears not shed
Distilled by deepest sighs and prayers.

If only we could bear the glaring shade,
Mark the rainbows in our eyes,
Illustrate the bluebells before they fade,
Share our fears, express our cries,
Then we might find the heaven we seek.
Among the upturned roots he fell asleep,
Labyrinthian hide that friends could find,
A bramble-den where fallen willows weep.
We carry what he left behind,
The brief portfolio of love.

Gethsemane shows us the most significant one who drinks from the cup of grief, the cup of ultimate testing. Jesus the pain-bearer drinks from it for all of us. He bears our separations, our forsakenness, our grief, our loneliness in his own body 'on the tree'. He bears the sins of the whole world. In this sense he is the scapegoat. Just as the goat is sent running to escape into the wilderness carrying the sins of the people, so Jesus takes our desert-pain into his own wilderness. He suffers on our behalf and in so doing feels the separation and alienation caused by our self-centredness.

The cries on the cross demonstrate this pain-bearing. He who is the living water thirsts; he who has spent a life of reconciling people to each other sees the disciple without a mother, a mother without a son. The point of the spear is one more dart of injustice into his side. He suffers the slings and arrows, not of outrageous fortune, but of those who feel their power is threatened by his power – the ultimate power of love. He bears the nails on the cross until his mission is accomplished, until that for which he came into the world, bearing the pain of sin, is complete. The doubting Thomas of our time will not believe in the pain-carrying ability of the Church until he can see its nail prints and thrust a hand into its wounded side.

A creative artist working with stitch and textiles recalls how she was so incensed by the graphic report of Bosnian women being raped that she wove a Bosnian Christa around the atrocities. She says, 'It took the rapes of the women of Bosnia and my little attempt to understand their suffering for me to look at the Passion in a new way. What the Christa demonstrates to me is that God is vulnerable, like me. That God, like women, is sometimes overpowered, bears incredible pain, dies at the hands of powerful people, and at the time of the pain and the death cannot do anything about it.'

When we talk about the vulnerability of God we are painting a picture which is far removed from the God who rules through Christ in majesty, who is the Christus Victor, subjugating all the forces in high places under his feet. Here we see the vicarious God who takes on himself suffering he does not deserve, the sins of others. He exposes himself to ridicule, taunting, false accusation, denial, rejection, betrayal, desertion and final alienation and forsakenness.

Whatever else Christian theology comes up with to try and explain suffering in the world, at least here we see the example of the God who incarnates himself, bears the worst that humanity can throw at him and makes the process redemptive. 'By his stripes we are healed.' He is not a remote God who watches from the sky the strange antics of humans demonstrating their inhumanity to one another. He actually bears our sins; he is the High Priest who carries the pains of separation with him.

Any theology of pain-bearing, therefore, must include the motif of the mediator. Jesus is the one who intercedes on our behalf. He is high and lifted up, mediating between a good God and a crucifying world, but he is also stretched out laterally – his compassionate arms are nailed to a cross reaching sideways to the thieves who die with him. 'He was wounded for our transgressions, he was bruised for our iniquities and by his stripes we are healed.'

This vicarious suffering and pain-bearing acts as a model for Christian redemptive ministry. It has the power to help us face the pain of the world and feel it. We come to Christ the pain-bearer, admitting that we are weary and heavy-laden. We come to find rest but we also come to find the strength to go on carrying our crosses and, despite the temptation to run away, to be lifted up by the one who shows us his scarred hands and feet.

Martin Eggleton

. . . There is still crisis and hurt and pain, even in spring. There is still some loneliness and depression at times, even in spring. There are still some questions, even in spring. There is still, at times, frustration with God, myself and the world, even in spring. And sometimes I feel like giving up, even in spring. But I don't.

I want to share so much more, but some things are best understood by being experienced personally . . . Healing thrives in sincere desperation.

God bless those of you still in that place of barren winter. I pray the Holy Spirit will show you God's gutsy love. May you meet Jesus, who is dying to heal, and may you grow into spring.

Nancy Ann Smith

* * * * *

I am not reduced to silence by the darkness. Job 23:17

* * * * *

*I have strength for anything through him
who gives me power.* Philippians 4:13

* * * * *

What if the thing we are meant to learn about God is that he is a waiting, suffering God who is acted upon rather than acts? Is there some truth here that we've lost? Are we so upset about suffering because we are so busy and activist and obsessed with solving problems that we have not waited long enough to expose ourselves to the scandalous truth about the meaning of suffering? Is suffering, submission to necessity, the carrier of redemption? And is redemption experienced *within* the suffering rather than in being rescued *from* the suffering?

Richard Holloway

Those who trust in the Lord for help
will find their strength renewed.
They will rise on wings like eagles;
they will run and not get weary;
they will walk and not grow weak.

Isaiah 40:31

Tired
And lonely,
So tired
The heart aches,
Meltwater trickles
Down the rocks,
The fingers are numb,
The knees tremble.
It is now,
Now, that you must not give in.

On the path of the others
Are resting places,
Places in the sun
Where they can meet.
But this
Is your path,
And it is now,
Now, that you must not fail.

Weep
If you can,
Weep,
But do not complain
The way chose you —
And you must be thankful.

Dag Hammarskjöld

There is a grace in things, even the darkest things, to which we need to keep open. When you are feeling down and you go to the eucharist, even though negative prayers are supposed to be unintelligent, it is good to ask for grace not to resist the grace that is there, to be as relaxed as possible and ready to accept the invisible, impalpable help that is certainly being given. Which is, like all sacramental moments, a representative image of the real presence in every moment.

When we have done what we can, some improvement may be clear, but not all will be set right; there will also be some failure, some remaining difficulties. We have to make the best of this residuum. In it there is always some good, there is the grace of what good it can bear. It is the grace of God.

Henry James would not be considered Christian in any formal sense, but he was in at the deep end of this truth when, in a letter to a friend grieving over the death of Rupert Brooke, among the tenderest condolences he wrote:

> All my impulse is to tell you to entertain the pang and taste the bitterness for all they are 'worth' – to know to the fullest extent what has happened to you and not miss one of the hard ways in which it will come home.

To see in some such way that the pang and bitterness of painful experience are not negative, not simply the violence of life and the heart's impoverishment under it, but that something precious is given in them that reaches us in no other way, so that it would be wisdom to go through with them, feeling them 'for all they are worth' – that is to be not far from the kingdom of God.

J Neville Ward

Sheila Cassidy writes – I like to think of our lives as being in the shape of a cross.

The upright – we can call it the vertical component – is man's relationship to God, his response to the first and greatest commandment of all:

> *You shall love the Lord your God with all your heart and with all your soul and with all your strength.*

This upright beam, then, is our prayer life.

The crossbeam – the horizontal component – is man's relationship with his neighbours: his response to the second commandment which is 'like unto the first':

> *You shall love your neighbour as yourself.*

Perhaps one of the greatest difficulties of the committed Christian is working out what is, for him, the correct balance between these two dimensions of his life. There is a very real sense in which we can never solve this problem because the more we pray the more we realise our need to pray, and the more we pour ourselves out for the hungry and the oppressed the more we feel called to serve. I have found my own answer to this problem, in so far as there is an answer, in a consideration of the mechanics of the cross.

Now, if a cross has a slender upright, the cross-beam it carries must be proportionately slender.

If we gradually increase the weight of the cross-beam, that is, if we try to carry a heavier and heavier load of social action on a weak prayer life, our cross will hold together for a while –

but there will come a time when the strain is too great – and the whole structure will buckle and fall. I believe that this happens to many people who are able to do great things for a while and then, because they are running on their own energy, 'burn out'. If, however, we make the upright of our cross

immensely strong and solid, if our prayer life is unshakeable and deeply rooted, then we shall find that we are able to support a broad and heavy crossbeam, that we can bear the weight of our neighbour's pain and suffering, steadily, day by day, because it is not we who are carrying the load, but God.

Lord, the pious words
of righteous people
don't always ring a bell with me.
Faced with the pain of suffering,
disappointment, damaged hopes,
whether it's my pain or another's,
I find it hard to hear it said
that God knows best.

I know you do,
but to load responsibility on you,
to imply that, somehow,
that makes it right and proper
that people suffer,
isn't a satisfying answer.

And when, sometimes,
I shout to you out loud,
the answer that I get
is deafening silence.
That's not so helpful either.
Then, I'm thrown back upon myself,
and see my own vulnerability.
And out of that grows prayer.
Because it's only out of need
that real prayer comes.
Or so it seems.

The cut worm, the pruned branch,
both bleed, each in its own way.
And in the bleeding lies its healing.
Lies new growth.
One of the many miracles of daily life.

Lord, when I scream,
and others too,
gather us to yourself.
Help me to see, and them,
that understanding isn't all that matters.
Isn't at the root of things.
The truth is,
that when I'm grafted into you,
my pain is your pain.
My groan your groan.
And your healing is mine.
In time.
And in eternity.

Eddie Askew

SHARING YOUR PAIN

We have shared in other people's experiences of pain-bearing within these pages and may well have seen something of our own pain-bearing reflected there. We have heard how different people have found support in their particular need or how they have simply struggled on 'staying with' the pain. Our utter dependence on God's strength and love as support and refreshment has been referred to again and again. But so often this love reaches out to us through the ministry of others and at times we need to ask for help and not to feel that we have failed in any way if we acknowledge that, for this time at least, we cannot continue on our own.

If you feel that it would be a relief to share whatever particular pain you may be bearing with someone else there are suggestions included concerning ways in which the Church wants to make this easy for you. In the ordinary course of events we all need to share our pain, our tiredness, our fears or doubts with at least one other person from time to time, but it is often most difficult to do so when our need is greatest. So it is hoped that the following possibilities will enable you – either now or at some time in the future – to find the right person with whom to share whatever you need to in total confidence.

* * * * *

- It is hoped that you will be able to find support from your Chairman of District, or within your Circuit staff meeting, or by contacting the two named ministers, Frances Young and Brian Fitzpatrick.

- Methodism also has close links with the Baptist Union Ministerial Counselling Service. This provides accredited counsellors throughout England and Wales (though unfortunately not yet in Scotland) and the contact names are –
  Michael Bray – 0181 699 4140 (home)
  0181 778 8601 (church)
  Tony Noles – 01277 840675

- The National Retreat Association, to which the Methodist Retreat Group is affiliated, has names of spiritual directors who would be glad to help –
  National Retreat Association, The Central Hall, 265 Bermondsey Street, London SE1 3UJ

- A new project, 'Cambridge Resources for Ministry – Sharing The Journey' seeks to provide support and pastoral care for those in ministry, both lay and ordained. Although able to assist at times of crisis, the main aim of the project is to enhance and maintain healthy patterns of life and work.

This is done through skilled listening and regular supervision, enabling ministers to avoid burn-out, to be renewed in their faith and sense of vocation, and to face the challenge of new directions in their calling. The intention throughout is to provide the kind of support which will build self-esteem and give ministers the confidence to assess options and alternatives, both for themselves and for those in their pastoral charge. This can provide the opportunity to review pastoral situations, with all their complexities of role, responsibility, emotion and dependency, before they become fraught. Staff teams can be enabled to reflect together on developing relationships of mutual support.

The project recognises the additional stress created by bereavement or marital crisis in the minister's own family, or by a work-load including a large proportion of people in acute need. The project is building a team of people who are willing to accept referrals in their own areas of experience, ranging from spiritual direction to congregational trauma. Where necessary, counselling can be offered by a BAC accredited counsellor.

In order to cover costs, there is a basic fee for each consultation. If you would like more information about the

project, please contact the Rev Joy Levine, 23 Newmarket Road, Cambridge CB5 8EG.
Initial telephone enquiries welcomed between 9.15am and 10.00am weekdays (01223 353393).

- Our friends are often the best sharers of our burdens. We do not always find it easy to be as honest with them about our inner pain as they would hope we would feel free to be. The grace implicit in shared friendship is often our most healing way forward, as this Jewish prayer so beautifully expresses –

> *Let there be love and understanding among us;*
> *let peace and friendship be our shelter from*
> *   life's storms.*
> *Eternal God, help us to walk with good*
> *   companions,*
> *to live with hope in our hearts and eternity in*
> *   our thoughts,*
> *that we may lie down in peace and rise up*
> *to find our hearts waiting to do your will.*
> *   Amen.*

ACKNOWLEDGEMENTS

Ray S Anderson	*The Gospel According to Judas,* Hilmers & Howard.
Eddie Askew	Many Voices, One Voice, *Facing The Storm*, The Leprosy Mission International.
Derek Bird	Cover photograph.
Sheila Cassidy	*Sharing the Darkness,* Darton, Longman & Todd. *Prayers for Pilgrims,* HarperCollins.
Jim Cotter	*Healing – More or Less,* Cairns Publications.
Charles Elliott	*Praying through Paradox,* HarperCollins.
David Fleming	*The Spiritual Exercises of St Ignatius,* The Institute of Jesuit Sources.
Alan Gaunt	*New Prayers for Worship,* John Paul the Preacher's Press.
Richard Holloway	*Paradoxes of Christian Life and Faith,* Mowbray.
Elizabeth Jennings	*Moments of Grace,* Carcenet.
Eugene C Kennedy	*The Pain of Being Human,* Albatross. Lion.
Ann Lewin	Poems from *Candles & Kingfishers* 11, Sirdar Road, Portswood, Southampton, SO2 3SH An extended account of Ann Lewin's experience of Mothercare will be found in *Life Cycles: Women and Pastoral Care* ed. Graham & Halsey, SPCK.
Henri Nouwen	*A Cry For Mercy,* Doubleday.
Sister Olga	Convent of St John the Baptist, Windsor.
Margaret Pizer	'Strength' from *To you the living,* Pinchquto Press, Sydney.
Jan Sobrino and Livro de Cantos	*Bread for Tomorrow* SPCK/Christian Aid.
Margaret Spufford	*Celebration,* Collins Fount.
Cecily Taylor	'Tears', *Liturgy of Life,* NCEC.
R S Thomas	'Groping' – *Later Poems,* Papermac, Macmillan.
Bernard Thorogood	A Restless Hope – *URC Prayer Handbook* 1995.
Jean Vanier	*The Broken Body,* Darton, Longman & Todd.
Denis Vernon	*Dawn to Dusk,* Methodist Publishing House.
Ken Walsh	*After the Dark,* SCM Press.
Neville J Ward	*Beyond Tomorrow,* Epworth Press.
Philip Yancey	*Where is God When it Hurts?,* Marshall Pickering. HarperCollins.